musings of a teenage soul

AISHVARYA PARAMESWAR IYER

contents

the phoenix in me

sometimes i look into the mirror and find a
girl from my past staring right back at me.
she looks worn out, with a burnt-up self-esteem,
a bruised soul, and voices inside her head;
that discourage her, ridicule her at every step;
that make her hate herself for being an epitome
of loyalty and truthfulness; that make her
forget that she is unique and worthy.

i watch as she gets dragged, into an abyss of
hate and chaos, ignited by a raging fire fuelled
by self-doubt and shame. i feel her pain as she
burns in the flames, her frail body crumbling
into ashes. i hear the surroundings echo
with laughter as people celebrate her downfall,
forgetting the blood, sweat and tears
she shed to heal their ailing hearts.

but then the laughter stopped and their joy
turned into shock; the flames died down
to reveal the girl rising out of the ashes,
wiser, braver and stronger than before.
at that moment, i smiled for i knew
that the phoenix in me would rise up
from the ashes each time someone
pulled her down, and refuse to give up
until she attained the zenith of her life.

cotton candies and ferris wheels

you are six, a wee little child
hiding behind the *pallu* of the
six yards draped around your
mother's body, staring at the
saccharine cotton clouds on
display in front of a giant wheel
with cabins hung upon its
paint-chipped circumference,
ascending towards the ether
at every quarter of an hour.

yesterday, teacher told your
class the earth was a large
ball rotating around itself.
what she forgot to mention
was that the world revolves around
confusion, which is why you
don't understand when mother
asks you to choose between
chewing on a cloud and traveling high
enough to seemingly hold one
between the tips of your nimble fingers.

your vision begins to blur as
realization pours a bucket of
water on your greased scalp,
you wanted both didn't you?
but on your mother's palm
rests a crumpled currency
note, a hearty meal compromised
for ten minutes of bliss you'll
forget about two years later.

i don't blame you, we're merely
kids in search of better days
when we can soar high up in the air
with rosy sweetness clutched
between our palms, nurturing cavities
between screams of excitement,
that slips away when we puke
our guts out on solid ground.

but for now we bite our lips
and stare longingly through
our saline-coated visions at the
joyrides we're going to miss out on
in exchange for a bubbly cloud
on wooden sticks that suddenly seems
too bittersweet to taste good anymore.

we were mellow pollens

we were mellow pollens on the
ochre tips of blooming flowers
when we mastered the art of
running away, from the winds
that led us astray, from the
breeze meant to lead us onwards.

we blossomed on the moss-glazed,
deserted corners of rundown
alleyways damp with tears,
nursing sage green wounds that
emerged on our spines, for all valiant
thorns prick their own stems in the wind.

we grew in and out, of each
other and the world because
we remained too young to
comprehend the decisions
we took in our utopian daze.
our lives have always been an us against
the world trope; we survived as long
as we had someone to hold onto.

but long gone are the days of
spring when love blossomed
in the air, now the chilling frost
nestled in our lungs melts our
insides, until we are hollow shells
huddled against stone cold walls

for our love was glazed eyes;
empty hearts; purchasing happiness
from shopping aisles, drinking
dopamine from glasses when our
vocal cords were parched from
screaming; because silence on the
other end equated another loss too
burdensome for our weary hearts.

so now we scream and cry and
yell, at ourselves and the world
to ignore the way those strings snap
between our fingers; instead
holding onto the faintest threads
of hope dangling in front of us.

children of the forest

the world thinks we are a rainbow
born out of sunlight on forest dew,
beautiful from afar, but meant to
disappear in due course beneath the
sloppy footprints left behind on soft
forest floors when people trod too
hard on ley lines glowing across
our bodies in muted hues, like fireflies
circling sal trees in broad daylight.

but we are the fresh dew drops sinking
into the dry corneas that stare too hard at
the crimson sunrise to soak in its
effervescent glow; washing away
the silvery dust lingering on dried
barks of trees whose rings speak more
volumes than thread-bound botany
books deserted on wooden library shelves.

we are the young kids with mystical orbs
concealed behind charcoal-rimmed
frames larger than our faces, with
our muddled brains buried in the fragrant
pages of fantasy novels; whose mellow
hearts clutch onto the sweet smells of
childhood like lilac cotton candy and
moss beds damp after gentle showers.

we are the ones who whisper lullabies
into the dainty ears of offsprings resting
on brittle branches, warding off the
nightmares poaching upon their blissful sleep.
we are the ones who stay hidden in
the shadows at dooms hour
on moonlit nights to protect the magic
nestled in the lush evergreen leaves
with small, leather-bound weapons
clenched in our pale fisted palms.

we are the children of the forest,
and we live and breathe our existence
becoming one with the trees, the breeze
and everything that fostered within us
this illusive sense of peace.

the ruined kids of this block

we are the ruined kids living in
three bhk homes on this block,
whose existence is
served with overcooked meat
and week-old take-aways at
dinner when conversations seem
to fade away like the nimble threads
connecting torn marriages.

our scrapped hands covered with
yellow paint and mouth sewed shut
by ruined eulogies are frowned
upon by full-throated, manicured,
self-proclaimed activists clad in
ripped *banyans*, who preach
hygiene and obedience despite
their flaxen medieval appearance.

flamboyant ringtones greet our
ears at six in the morning from
windows that stink of late night
frat parties and coercion excused
in the name of fun and drunkenness,
while their residents serenade us
with pick me smiles and renditions
of "april come, take this heart away"
even though it's autumn, not spring.

not so covert stares and whispers
trail behind us like faithful companions
when grocery runs seem too intimidating
for our timid brains to accomplish.
however, the moment we walk away
their jeers spill out in
full force like split plastic packs;
calling us the ruined kids of this block,
for we never fit the meagre
standards of living set by them.

[*because we never attempted to,*
because we never wished to]

rebellion buried by molten hands

we live in rundown cities where poems scribbled
by the youth collapse into a mirage of endless blue
floating beneath deserted lands, glistening with
mineral salts pouring out of pain-stricken irises;
echoing caves sealed behind lips; jaws silenced,
aching from
attempts at breaking apart the thick hides of
patriarchy force-fed by coarse fingers dipped in
honey-coated misogyny; after all sugar isn't healthy
for their diabetic hearts.

we build our abodes on abandoned cemeteries with
coal furnaces to defrost a numbness we cannot feel
for we are four feet away from falling six feet too
deep to climb back up by ourselves. our wilted palms
clutch onto silvery-silt slipping away from the cracks
between our fingers to soak in the warmth of a
presence left unsung among the ashes.

our molten skins commence burning at daybreak
when we step out without lathering sufficient
sunscreen to ward off the radiation emanated by
sleazy pupils wearing robes of lust and greed. their
pride transforms into fiery vexation the moment
denial rolls out of our lacerated tongues that speak
foreign dialects often misunderstood by uniformed
superintendents dipping their tea bags in sugar free
soy milk, who will never experience the need to wear
sunscreen in their lives.

so we write poems on torn scraps of papers with
pungent ink and ignite them on ceremonial furnaces
so they collapse into a grey mass and float away from
the peering orbs of patriarchy, hiding soft fruits of
our rebellion beneath the sands, to be unearthed by
someone whose singed skin has been built out of a
little more courage than our feeble hearts.

your local, rebellious teen rants

"INCREASING CASES OF TEENAGERS BEING DIS…"

awfully chopped newspaper scraps rest on
paint-splashed plywood, their snobby headlines
screaming at my 'insolence' in a size 20 rouge
gothic script highlighted in bold.
a sans serif font and tinted doodles exhibit my
'hostile tendencies and mood swings' as if i
were a subject of experimental interest existing
purely to cater to elite discussions of the
educated at breakfast on sundays.

my 'guilty pleasures' are apparently worse than
the remnants of their cigars rolling around on
ash trays for weeks and the pungent stench of
liquor shops lingering on shirts when they return
home on days of hard(ly) work. my existence
has been stripped bare and laid out like a pack
of cards being shuffled every fifteen minutes in front
of stalls outside offices on weekdays, bustling to life
with lewd dealings and vile conversations that make
bile rise up my clogged oesophagus.

i'm supposed to be appalled by this, aren't I? -
the casual snide remarks, the over exaggerated
statements, futile opinions of learned folks;
all of this is supposed to give me a headache,
make me crumble down into pieces so that
they can fit me into rusted cages that stink of
godawful prejudices and baseless stereotypes.

but i don't care anymore; their bold headlines
have been reduced to torn scraps that decorate
the signs I hold up in my rebellion.
their agitated voices fall on flat ears,
serving as inspiration to create revolution and
their flustered hoaxes at self-redemption lie
amidst the trash i discard each day.

i don't care about them, i choose to be
the *"disrespectful, disinterested, dysfunctional, distant..."*
teenager they label me as, whose existence
has been degraded too many times to fit the pages
of a dreadful newspaper when they run out of
content to publish. i refuse to care about their
hypocrisy,
their insecurities and their opinions for they refuse
to empathise and recognize me for being human
and struggling to live a life imposed on me by
everyone else.

who is the real monster?

once upon a time, when society was struck by
boredom in the midst of watching power dynamics
and hierarchies flip the lives of people upside down,
it sought to create another
peculiar technique, where it classified chosen few as
spawns of the devil.

it started off as a light joke, passed from one ear
to another over drinks in between ball dances and
courtships. it was whispered behind closed curtains
and shut doors of ancestral mansions where honour
and traditions were irreversible laws. it resonated
in the air as cruel hands pushed out innocent lads
to live on rough asphalt roads one freezing night
just because they couldn't bring themselves to meet
their eyes.

*"you are a monster, an abomination, a disgusting soul
never supposed to be born."*

but was that child a monster when you crushed
their fragile heart and mocked them for dreaming
of something more than what they were 'supposed'
to? was that child a monster when you leashed their
bodies and forced them into cages too small to fit

their growing limbs? was that child the real monster when you refused to accept how different they were from the rest of the world? i think not.

so next time society advises you in its crooning voice dipped in malice, *do not fraternise with those monsters, or else you'll become one too*", stare right back at their spiteful orbs and tell them that there are no monsters in this world, only those who are repulsive enough to label others as one.

home is where the heart is

you ask me if i'd run away with you one evening, i say
yes, i would.

so we sneak out after supper in search of an abode
beyond these ancestral walls, in search of a place
where we could bare our souls naked without
worrying about being stabbed in the back by those
with whom we share our blood. we don't turn
around as we steal the key to unlock the doors to
freedom, climb up the giant gateways and leap into
the unknown, moments before the guards rouse from
their mid-chore slumber.

we trudge through the sombre-green woods with
lofty homes hanging snugly above our heads, we
plough through the sweeping meadows, plucking
daisies and petunias that decorate its well-worn
edges, we toil through the lanes of the sultry
countryside, holding hands with the wind and kissing
a trespasser or two while swallows and bluebells
serenade us overhead.

we keep striding along, two wild heirs without a
care for worldly matters, leave alone hierarchies and
politics, in search of a dwelling that sings rhapsodies
of home. as the sun's lids droop on the horizon, we
abandon everything that we were taught to respect
to unfold a life we could live for ourselves, with no
bonds to hold us back.

if my pen could speak

if my pen could speak,
it would talk to the world
about the long hours
when i'd sit on my chair
and twirl it between my fingers,
looking for inspiration to write.

if my pen could speak,
it would tell the world,
about the fantasies i'd create in my head.
it would share anecdotes of me,
who has lived fourteen years,
lost in the realm of her dreams.

if my pen could speak,
it would laugh and tell the world
about those days when i'd write and
rewrite something for the umpteenth time,
only to end up using the phrases
i had initially planned.

if my pen could speak,
it would tell the world,
about those pieces of poetry
built upon my insecurities,
that concealed a saga
of surging emotions
from the rest of the world.

if my pen could speak,
it would tell the world,
about those innumerable instances
where i looked down upon myself.
it would share stories
of shame and disappointment
that still remain sore spots for me

that is why i sincerely wish
that my pen would never learn
how to speak to the world,
in order to protect all those sentiments
i wish to keep buried within me forever.

why I can't I write my heart out?

in front of my eyes
lies a blank sheet of paper
that refuses to fill
no matter how hard i try.
each time, i ask myself;
why can't i inscribe
my thoughts into words?

i spend hours mulling over
each phrase in my poems,
yet when i'm done,
something's always missing,
and i'm compelled to write
each word, each stanza
all over again;
why can't i get myself
to appreciate what I've written?

i keep trying even though
my hands begin to ache,
my pen runs out of ink,
my mind blanks out.
yet, i can never write
and tell the world
what keeps weighing down my mind;
why i can't i write my heart out?

quarantine blues

cobalt beams from the laptop screen strike
my purblind eyes as i wake up from my slumber
in the middle of a zoom meeting, the cerulean glare
as reprimanding as my teacher when
she finds me decorating the last few pages of my
notebook with artistic inscriptions during her in-class
sermon on the profoundness of renaissance artists.

months ago, her words would have irked my ego
more than i'd like to admit, but having experienced
waves of summer depression, i can't help but feel that
being reprimanded for not paying attention would be
heaven compared to solitary confinement in my
room,
staring at overheated device screens for more than a
year.

now, i'd trade all the time in the world to spend
fifteen minutes in a classroom where i don't analyse
sullen expressions captured by a webcam;
where my stellar scribbles gain their rightful
attention;
where i no longer calculate screen times (and ignore
them)

while writing poems to prevent further damage
to my depreciating eyesight,
and the only blues i cared about was the colour of
the sky when i travelled to and fro from school;
i am sick and tired of these quarantine blues.

on speaking to someone after an era of silence

something about awkward conversations makes me
feel like i swallowed too much cream cake in a single
sitting to commemorate all the celebrations i missed
because I was stuck inside the faded lime yellow walls
of my bedroom.

my maroon-tinted nails hover above the neon green
call button next to a name i would yell every three
minutes back when high school felt like a fever
dream, as if pressing it would cause a chemical
explosion in our dingy laboratory.

i think back to the times when conversations between
us flowed like the honey i drizzle on pancakes at
breakfast to replace the bottles of maple syrup that
never came home, because foreign shipments were
stopped in some city abroad whose name i cannot
pronounce.

a few months ago, my notifications were alive with
texts i received from your end. now i no longer recall
the sound of your voice cracking when you laughed
at horrible puns till tears streamed down your cheeks;
and tickled me till i did the same.

i've not seen you for you for so long, i wonder if you
still remember complaining about how sensitive
your cheeks felt when i pulled them for too long and
threw a tantrum till i compromised and fed you *aloo
parathas* and *achar* mom used to pack for lunch.

you've every right to be upset with me, i've ghosted
you for months, effectively spoiling all the virtual
movie night plans we made so we could stay up till
four thirty to watch the sunrise on our roofs and
sleep in till late afternoon post that.

although i abhor admitting it, a large chunk of my
heart misses your irritable presence screaming off-
tune bollywood numbers in my ear when i wanted to
sleep through bus journeys back home, so much that
i'm willing to bear an awkward first conversation.

so, i hurriedly press the obnoxious button and ignore
my haphazard heartbeats as your ringtone blares
through the silence, *once, twice, thrice,* till i hear your
familiar laugh answer the phone, *"hello stranger, it's
been a long time since we last spoke huh?"*

someday we will all be lonely trains traveling through the night.

paan-stained cement platforms
of the local station have a
peculiar stench that reminds me
of all the odysseys i bypassed
because i was too young and
intimidated by the unknown that
lay beyond the brick walls of
our homes in a forgotten town.

but now as i stand too close to
the edge, peering down at the
packets of snacks and ten rupees
plastic bottles squashed and
crumpled next to the alloyed steel
i can't help but think of how life
would be if i shed my
jacket of comfort four years ago
and stood here all alone, waiting
for trains that never come because
they're stuck at a foothill miles away,
too weary to make a steep climb.

the night feels drowsy under my skin,
but all signs of exhaustion seem
to exit as the rumbling horns
ricochet in the distance, disturbing
the stillness of the night, wheels
clacking and vibrating through my
calcium deficit bones, carrying the
burden of a few hundred lives.

weary arms arouse from their
power naps to crowd together,
holding onto the frayed straps
of battered luggages in more shapes
than what you could possibly
identify in a math textbook.
people rush to and fro all around,
securing a last cup of tea, a toilet
break or a hurried hug from wailing,
wrinkled palms before fighting
for their early boarding rights.

the beaming headlights grin at
me, blinding my pupils with their
infectious zeal minutes before
midnight, and i wonder if its smile
is so luminescent to conceal the fact
that its faded armour isn't made
of coarse aluminium but brittle

loneliness from traversing
the highs and lows of the
tumultuous journey on its own,
hearing the sound of frolic
and laughter echo through
rundown corridors full of life.

and so, i spend the rest of my
sundown journey staring at a glassy
orb play hide and seek in the
smoggy ether, angst sedimenting
heavily in my chest as i think about
a day when i would be a lonely train
drifting into the obscure night,
leaving behind all sense of home and
familiarity in search of a town
whose station lights glimmer faintly
in the distant horizon.

on why natural disasters have human names

once upon a time, back in the days
when i'd hide beneath my bedframe
each time earthquakes shook my home,
(and consequently, my own sanity)
my elders told me that most dangerous
calamities arose from human emotions.
now, i finally understand why they said it.

our ancestors were god fearing mortals
who surmised natural disasters to be
vicious retributions for the sins
they committed in their lifetimes.
they chastised themselves,
performed severe penance,
but were incapable of calming the
fearsome whirlwind raging in their minds.

their stormy spirits were flooded by
tsunamis of explosive emotions,
the blood in their veins boiled like lava
flowing through volatile volcanoes,
their orbs were the eyes of hurricanes
that remained pacific watching the world
being wreaked by tempestuous chaos.

our ancestors feared catastrophes,
they were scared of pain and death,
they feared their almighty gods,
but above all, they feared the evil
lurking in their spirits that gave rise
to sentiments that could destroy us all.
so, they gave natural disasters human
names, because they are an
amalgamation of these sentiments;
destructive, wild and volatile, like
the people who chose to name them.

on the deficiencies in your bones

there's a small spot on the inner crevice of your left elbow that seems to ignite when you rub it too hard to remove indents of all the times pointy syringes were pierced into your skin at six in the morning to measure quantities you knew you were lacking.

test reports that arrive hours late(r) are dressed in cream and orange uniforms, safeguarding printed pages with negative numbers, that reiterate results you are aware of deep within your bones because you quiver each time you stand on your feet for too long.

your insecurities are forged in the heart of the marrow and course through your blood, holding onto the overburdened sleeves of the cells it manufactures, occasionally nabbing away the nutrients they carry to strengthen your withering immunity.

you wonder why you haven't ruptured your anatomy and hurt yourself with its splinters yet, but tensile objects like you that are calcium deficit and built out of worthlessness don't leave behind shards to commemorate themselves, they are subdued and simply fade away into a void of non-existence.

your faith in a puny being like yourself is unhealthy,
for eventually there'll come a day when even you
won't be unable to cover up for the all times you've
tripped accidentally. so please stop being careless and
pay heed to yourself, because i don't know if your
bones can hold you up for much longer now.

*[because frankly i don't know if anybody wants to keep
holding up someone who remembers them only when
they know there's no one else they can rely upon in this
world]*

a museum at midnight

moonlight seeps into my room
through the gap between my curtains
and casts a pale, eerie glow that makes
tiny specks of dust break dance at midnight.

the luminescence accentuates the
cracks on the walls, and segregates the
rightful territories of spiders and lizards
like boundaries on the world map.

the dolls on my bed have sombre eyes
at daytime; but the moment the sun sets,
they remind me of *annabelle*, who now
rests under lock and key in a box at a museum.

the pencil shavings on my study table
are all artifacts in their own rights;
talk to them at night, and they'll tell you about
my trait for preserving fragmented things.

the dustbin beside the table lies empty
all day long, i find the 'trash' in my room
too precious to be discarded away; maybe
i could give *nonseum* a run for their money?

the bookshelves, and my woollen blanket
have more history than the priceless artefacts
used by medieval kings, but i conceal this fact
so they can't be taken away to be displayed
in the glass shelves of some foreign museum.

by now, the moonlight illuminates
each room in my house, but my inclination
for languidness beats my desire to look for
heirlooms hidden in the crevices of those walls,
so i leave those antiques buried
in their rightful spots tonight and decide
to dig them out and chronicle their tales
during my quest on another moon-lit night.

10:10 monologues of a
broken clock

(non) rhythmic beats pulse through
my brass anatomy, their vibrations
driving my divergent arms to
oscillate around the periphery
of my dust-laden skin in a manner
that (no longer) remains the only
constant in my life, presently hanging
by a nail on the chipped surface
of soot-stained walls.

my daily pleas are drowned beneath
the yelling voices of salarymen
thirty seconds late for their nine to five
jobs on monday mornings because
the tainted scars running across
my body no longer indicate my purpose
with accuracy, instead they remain
a sign of my inconsistency and failure
to dictate the truth binding all
life together with fractional threads
that seem to glow each second.

my arms shoot arrows that move in
tangents above the minds of seven
year olds who cannot distinguish
between twos and tens and prefer
the fancy neon numbers on digital
wrist dials, singing the stroke of an hour
in loud, melodious tunes till their
microchips fade into oblivion; much
after the lithium coursing through my
veins evaporates into thin air.

i don't blame them, after all there's
no one who understands the way
small drops of time converge to
form rivers spanning across the
millennium, leaving behind the small
shattered relics who crowned the
highest towers back in the days
than me, who now hangs on kitchen
walls as a mere aesthetic mantelpiece
occasionally serving the needs of those
from our days of youth who choose
to trust us despite their own misgivings,
simply because they cannot keep
up with the changing times read by
the curious eyes of this generation.

*[after all, time flows away with each passing second
and awaits no one, including us who kept track of its
activities all throughout our lives]*

it's 11-11 today, make a wish all day

i

twinkle twinkle little star, when i was young i often wondered how it would feel to be lost among the celestial crowd in the wee hours of night. the welkin is boundless and you're floating in space, light years away from those from those dearest to you. you seal your desolation, conceal it beneath your stellar semblance with dazzling smiles but when you're out in the limitless void all by yourself, staring at the gloom for aeons on end, cracks in your facade will shine through.

don't hide them please, let those rays refract through the dingy expanse and reach this realm with their lustrous siblings to prove that even the most effulgent stars have a side they're alarmed to show the world.

ii

i've always had a fuzzy memory of my days of oblivious innocence, but here's what i remember about those rare occasions when i wasn't building castles in mid-air or diving into evergreen novels; i yearned for a friend. i yearned for someone who'd understand my fascination for the twilight hours and the mythical beings that lived in jungles across my

gardens. i yearned for someone who'd be a silent,
luminescent ray when i wished to read in solitude
during the pitch dark of midnight.

i know you yearn for a friend just like i do and i hope
you don't stop yearning for them. light takes forever
to reach us, but when it does, it sets a *dazzilion* lives
aglow. your friends will do the same for you.

iii

there will times when your radiance would never
catch the eager eyes of kindergarten kids, and instead
meet a few grudging orbs. there will be occasions
when celestial storms would seem too harsh and
prolonged. hold on, don't give up just yet. you and i
may belong to distant millenniums but time remains
the thread of familiarity that binds us. so make a wish
list and wait for parallel junctures to arrive once again
and recite your dreams with a smile on your face.
soon enough life will seem astronomical once again.

and someday, when you grow old and weary and
descend from your empyrean abode in a gleaming
procession, I'll stand there on my rooftop and wave
at the skies, and make a wish to reconcile with you
one day.

a list of small moments in life

there's nothing more beautiful than the sound of the
breeze brushing past the branches of a willow tree,
swaying it gently so they dance in the moonlight to
the faint chirps of crickets concealed in dew-scented
moss beds, who witness this seraphic sight.

there's nothing more beautiful than caramel hands
colliding with sweat-drenched fingertips as they rush
to grab the choicest pieces of popcorn from the extra-
large tub resting in the awkward space between them
at the movies, causing pixeled flushes to erupt on the
apples of their air-conditioned cheeks.

there's nothing more beautiful than listless eyes
coming across a pair of focused orbs squinting at the
blackboard from across the classroom, grinning at
the manner in which their razor-sharp incisors chew
upon cheap five-rupee plastic pens and stain their
lower jaws with cerulean lip tint.

bear hugs and raspberry pecks envelop droopy morales in fluffed blankets knitted with comfort and affection to warm up those tired bones and rejuvenate them with love. after all, there's nothing more beautiful than the presence of someone who may not be able to solve your dilemmas, but makes life simple and much more beautiful for you.

ways in which i'm kind to myself

the half-full fancy ceramic cup at a cosy café two
blocks away from my three bhk apartment looks at
me with sugar doused eyes, begging to be reunited
with the hydrochloric acid bubbling in excitement in
my abdomen. i don't hold back my smile as i give my
endorphins a field trip today.

i have been blessed with permanently quivering
fingers that tremble and sob uncontrollably when
they see tasks piling up on my overcrowded desk. i
don't force obedience upon them, instead i give them
a break to recuperate so they could work happily the
next day.

beneath the philtrum of my lip rests a faint scar from
all the times i bit too hard to prevent my tear glands
from spilling emotional secrets. my incisors still
subconsciously close down upon them, but each bite
is a bit softer and moistened with saline to prevent
them from bruising anymore.

my thighs have always complained about trousers
that never seem to fit them very well. now i don't
stuff them in non-stretch elastics or doll them up for
others, i allow them the space to choose what they
wish to wear so they could be comfortable in their
own skin.

i've been practicing to roll my tongue the correct way
so the next time i speak, i don't stumble when i say
no and prioritize myself before helping those who say
they need me. at the end of the day, you can't be kind
to the world if you don't choose to dedicate small acts
of kindness towards yourself.

a listicle on love

love smells like petrichor soaking the atmosphere
after the first monsoon showers, arriving through
my drenched window during the last hours of dusk
to infuse my breath with fruitful promises of joyous
days yet to come forth.

love feels like a clement sensation oscillating in the
gentle breeze blowing past the *verandah* close to
6:00 pm each day, that makes my anatomy vibrate
seventy-two times in a minute as it brushes past my
cheekbones.

love tastes like puffed packets of sugar-loaded sweets
and savoury snacks melting on my tongue each time
my taste buds crave a delightful pampering to remove
the routine blandness of daily meals.

love sounds like the symphonic orchestra of chirps
echoing religiously at the crack of dawn and the
occasional sound of contagious laughter ringing
inside the dining halls on days when worries are
discarded outside the main door.

love grows between the wrinkles and lines on a
serene face blooming in all its glory, as it solaces
the world with gleeful smiles that spark joyous
revolutions, encompassing every aspect of our
mundane lives.

love, is *omnipresent* in every aspect of our life.

love is a pungent hoax

"you don't trust me"
"yes, i do"
"prove it".

our chapped lips meet in a passionate embrace in
a secluded corner behind the asphalt bricks of our
rusty school building, away from the discerning eyes
of teachers and students and surveillance cameras.

we kiss; the tangy essence of lemon pickles floods my
taste buds and for a moment, i get distracted from the
wave of emotions that threaten to flood my charcoal
orbs. i hold them in like i subdue my disgust for
pungent pickles, i'd eat bottles of them in a sitting if
that means i could love you forever.

warm wintry sunrays caress my back in comforting
motions, empathising with the turmoil inside my
head. it knows how difficult it is to love when you and
your heart are eclipsed in the shadows and cannot
shine beneath the same sky. but love wasn't meant to
be easy, was it?

i wonder why you trust 11:11 wishes, parallel lines separated by an indefinite space called time that never allow them to meet. i wonder why you trust the world more than a finite mortal who pines for you with every breath of her existence. i wonder why you don't trust me, even when i'm yours to see and feel and touch.

i can see the regret pooling in your eyes when we break apart from our kiss, it makes me feel like i've tainted your blood with sacrilege. but unlike you, i'm not afraid to bear the weight of a thousand sins, if that means I can profess our love in front of the world. for me, there's no greater joy than knowing i've fought till end just to spend these cherished moments with you.

i know you don't trust me, yet your faithless love is the only hoax i believe in. it wraps me in a cocoon of belongingness and makes me sail on clouds of euphoria. i can feel you hesitate each time we meet my love, i just wish you'd stop plucking the strings of my cardiac, swindle it with whimsical promises and make it play quaint melodies for every minute i breathe.

for i can delude my heart into believing you didn't adore me all this time we've been in love, but i can't live on knowing that you've never trusted me all throughout our lives.

the griefcase i carry to work is empty, except for my lonely heart

you once fell in love
with the idea of your name
on someone else's lips,
the shadow of your smile
contouring the bones of
their rouge-dusted cheeks
when you stroll around
the quadrangle at six p.m.,
fingers intertwined in feverish
embraces that leave your
palms perspiring for more

you live in square flats
with small bedrooms and
wide windows that can't
house the feelings drumming
through your cardiac when it
drums one-twenty beats in
a single minute.
so you confess your amour
through thirty-six syllables
stretched across a window pane.
[but not one of them is i love you.
because you *don't*.]

you don't love anyone,
not even yourself,
leave alone the sound of your
name on foreign lips that
trace growing pains
on the junctures of your bones
with tainted promises,
and numbness with
salivary grease drooling
down their pallid cheeks.

you don't love anymore,
instead you've built a home
that houses loneliness
and leaves you yearning
for companionship, and for
a love you'll never attain.

so you wake up at six
every morning and go to work
with a griefcase
clutched in your aching arms,
leaving behind a home
and a heart that houses
no one but (l)on(e)ly you

i hold my own hands because there is no one else to hold them for me

the ether seemed peculiarly gloomy that evening;
months of frustration drowning in a torrential
downpour, washing away the ground beneath our
revamped converses.
your bare fingers hold onto my jittery palms in an
embrace i believe is supposed to soothe my gut that
is presently fizzling like the soda you threw away
moments ago.

[*you said it was too pungent for your tongue, i wonder if
you'd say the same thing if our lips chanced to meet in
the rain*]

our fingers intertwine like sunrays in the morning,
warm enough to make my palms tingle delightfully;
so warm they begin to melt away and drip down on
the drenched pavement. yet i tighten my grip so i can
soak in the comfort your palms offer till a lopsided
grin decorates your face and your taunting rasp seeps
into my eardrums, "do you like holding my hand so
much?"

*[no, i mean yes, i like holding your hand, but to be
honest I am afraid you'll slip away from me if i don't
hold onto you tight enough]*

but i can't find any phrases to accessorize the
uncertainties drawing lines upon my skin, so i simply
hold on and soak in the sensations of my palms
heating up in decimal magnitudes, calluses brushing
against your knuckles, pressing the flesh in soft,
jagged motions as abandonment issues resurface
inside my head. your hands feel like the home i've
been looking for all this time. but unfamiliarity makes
you hesitant, so i hold back from holding your hands
the way i've been wanting to hold one my entire life.

*[besides you'd probably freak out, people love holding
hands, not holding on in order to not let you go]*

but you did let go of my hands five weeks after we
clicked this photo at the same spot in front of those
barren trees whose branches broke off in the snow-
storm the previous night due to the frozen weight
they couldn't shake off. now, i no longer hold hands
with people. instead i stare at the way my palms peel
off in winters, the way my nails break under the
slightest pressure, the way my fingers are crooked
and bent sideways at their joints and seem to fit
perfectly when i clasp them together.

*[i ignore the way they crave for touch, for warmth that
makes them melt, for comfort to hold onto, for I am
destined to hold my own hands forever]*

confessions of a dishevelled man sobering up

hurt. that's all i comprehend the moment i arouse from my stupor. hurt, that makes me feel like i consumed burning charcoal embers from the molten pits of an abyss and drowned my senses in its fiery lava. it hurts, it always does, so much i've grown accustomed to this pain. hurt feels like home now, the one i stumbled upon and refuse to leave, for there's nowhere else for me to go.

"last night was a mistake" that's what people usually say. but i've been tying sacred bonds and spilling heartfelt secrets to my guilt for countless nights; it is now more familiar to me than anyone i dare call a friend. guilt has taken up a permanent abode within my heart, without it i'd probably feel like shards of glass scattered on the floor after i smashed it on my 'friend's' head.

my memories are fuzzy, but again *i don't recall the last time i had a clear head.* all i know is that one moment i'm at the counter asking the bartender to open my tab and the next i'm on the receiving end of a bruising punch, lying on the floor with a sore jaw. i don't know what went down in the fight, but it must have been worth it since i felt something after so long.

i faintly recall the first time i had a sip of the devil's elixir, euphoria erupting within me, wishing bones writhing in shame at my incompetence. but i didn't care. all i wanted was to *forget forget forget*. forget everything and lose myself in the befuddlement that enveloped me with each sip till i sank into the depths of a murky pool of debt. it didn't hurt, i couldn't feel, and for a moment the high made me believe i was invincible.

but phantom pains linger in my liver, concealing themselves behind the adrenaline, emerging only when they know i'm high enough to push me off a cliff, back down to my fumbled senses. the pain never goes away, it sticks to me and grows, consuming and burning away the emotions i feel. hurt is all i comprehend but this time it doesn't feel like home. i don't want it anymore, i want to forget it. yet each time i fill my guts so there's no space left within me; the pain stays back for longer. *i don't know how to (not) feel it anymore.*

12:24 am angst songs

i often hunt for validation at 12:23 am in the wee
hours of morning when walls are silent and the lights
are dim enough for me to think back and wince at
how i slid down a flight of stairs six and half minutes
ago because i was adamant on trusting a pair of pupils
that cannot see without the assistance of flimsy
plastic frames.

my fingers occasionally slither towards the
switchboard cracked around the edges because i
don't know how to fix broken things despite my own
misgivings and refuse to call in extra help to repair
it. i should be able to do it, i should, (*but i can't, and
i refuse to admit it*) so i keep trying until my self-
esteem stoops down a couple more inches.

i observe the jagged lines close to the edged of ceiling
under aqua lights while i reminisce the palpitations
echoing through my anatomy when i held on to the
bedhead desperately to make the nightmares stop.
my smart watch tells me i have a faint heartbeat and
the last thing i remember before blacking out is hope,
that tomorrow it beats a little faster than yesterday.
(but it does not)

some part of me is weary of wishing, hates how hope
seeps into my lungs despite the no entry signs hung
up on the veins all across my body. i force myself to
cough it out the moment it reaches my airbags, but it
sticks to me like a pebble on foot soles, a nuisance i
can't manage to get rid of.

sixty seconds are enough for my mind to generate
diverging opinions about my ability to feel so it
bombards me with emotions just because i don't want
to feel anymore. yet, I cannot convince myself to
reproach it, numbness makes you grow desperate; for
pain, for yearning, for hurt that makes you resonate
with every sob song on your playlist.

[and so i spend three hours and thirty-six minutes
waiting for light to rise again at the end of the tunnel
and snatch away the solace that floats in the dim
silence, drowning my sentiments in heart-breaking
songs on loop for the umpteenth time this night.]

is anxiety just a silhouette or is it a part of me?

i can't believe you, *mirror mirror on the wall*, to think there'd come a day when i'd see these silhouettes staring back at me with smiles on their faces, smiles so sour they make my tear glands melt when i look at the jagged crevices of their chapped lips; lips that quiver before they utter a single syllable; syllables that when strung together form strange sentences playing hangman, hanging awkwardly in the air.

[none of this makes sense to you, it never did, it never will, but they don't make sense to me either]

i didn't know who they were, but they visited me at odd hours when i wished for solitude, refused to have a civil conversation, left before i could learn their names. they crowded around me, clogged my eardrums with their echoing rasps, but deserted me when i was in need of comfort to be whispered into these ears. they clutched my back so i couldn't move forward but let go of me when I had no one to fall back on. they were everywhere, but when i looked around, i was (*and still am*) all alone.

*[none of this makes sense to you, it never did, it never
will, but they don't make sense to me either]*

my friends keep telling me not to lag behind again,
but they can't see the extra baggage drooped over
my shoulders; they're invisible, invisible but so
overwhelming my knees give out and fall, meeting the
pavement in a bruising kiss. arms reach out; they hold
me down so all i can do is crane my neck, watch my
friends walk uphill, away from me, sharing snippets
I was never a part of; i don't want to lag behind, but
how do i climb up with a baggage so bulky it weighs
me down?

*[none of this makes sense to you, it never did, it never
will, but they don't make sense to me either]*

their visits have grown frequent these past few
months, maybe the loss of companionship hit them
hard as well? for a moment I believed we could be
cordial; they wouldn't petrify me anymore, i knew
them by now. but *mirror mirror on the wall*, why do
the silhouettes staring at me with their twisted smiles
look like me now? why do their quivering lips and
fumbling words sound like the monologues i've been
delivering all this time? why do these silhouettes
remind me of myself; frail, fatigued and flawed?

mirror mirror on the wall, if these silhouettes are part of me, does this mean i can't i make sense of myself anymore?

what anxiety tastes like

anxiety tastes like -

dingy roadside huts along rundown footpaths when
you travel a few miles too far away from your abode
and feel your enzymes throw tantrums at how aloo
parathas no longer retain same flavour that melts
on your tongue when you stuff too many pieces into
your mouth at Sunday brunch;

bland cereal turned soggy because you soaked it for
too long while scrambling through your morning
routine, and now choose to rush through your day
on a queasy stomach rumbling with fiery hunger that
is strong enough to make your quivering legs almost
collapse in the middle of a crowded street enroute the
bus stop;

sleepless nights when you're on a roller coaster ride
descending endlessly at two hundred miles per hour,
eyes squeezed shut, palms melting, silent screams
oozing out of your sore throat, crying futilely for help
you know will never arrive for you only travel on
empty rides;

words lodged in your windpipe that halt your breath
as your blurry vision tries to solve the mystery
behind lips moving silently, mumbling incoherent
words while sinewy arms grasp your shoulders and
shake you till you break out of your ill-timed stupor;

the metallic tinge lingering on your tongue when
you lick away the rouge droplets accumulating on
your fingertips despite your hemophobia because
you want to feel something immediately, *desperately*,
because you're so numb to everything except this
sinking feeling that is always drowning your lungs,
and seeping into your abdomen till you can digest
everything, regardless of whether or not it freezes
your heart or burns your skin.

[but even though I try to delude myself into
encapsulating what the lingering emotions taste like,
I know that anxiety tastes like me, because each time
i'm anxious, I cannot think, feel, hear or see]

an ode to liyue

miles away from the dandelion winds of freedom,
resting in the earthen valleys beyond the polar
mountains, rests a prosperous city in the land of
monoliths, whose name symbolizes the pricelessness
contained in each blade of rock you lay your hands
upon.

ochre hues adorn the atmosphere bustling with
culture and heritage passed down for millenniums. its
vast history is etched on the crux ships anchored in
the magnificent harbour that set sail to seven nations.
silken flowers and dainty lilies bloom like the trade
that flourishes all year round, igniting lives of merry
folk like lanterns floating in the twilight skies.

people of this city wear robes of wisdom, their
eyes twinkling with sparks of knowledge inscribed
in the ancient lore from days of the archon wars.
the diversity in their ethnicities births a savoury
cuisine that makes the weariest bellies dance in glee.
their integrity and zeal are etched in stone like the
contracts that bind them together to form a gleaming
star on the teyvat's map.

the blessings of morax shine upon the city, illuminating it with rainbows of affluence. the exquisiteness of the natural treasure, the bountiful presents that are in abundance like the currency, the vigour and vitality in people's eyes and their yearning for knowledge are but jade stones on the forged crowns of this beloved city of the east, that holds a treasured spot deep within my heart.

an ode to autumn

autumn sets in with a gusty breeze when the last of the rains wash away and leave behind an exquisite scent of petrichor as a souvenir for all the love stories that began on drenched afternoons beneath the pouring skies.

now, young romeos rewrite their own tragic fates by stealing raspberry kisses concealed in the branches of golden maned oak trees that drop comfort through dried brown leaves during auburn skied evenings on autumn roads.

a distinct chill lingers in the air, that waltzes with pearl-like droplets resting on the evergreen freshness waiting for stars to set on the crimson horizon at the onset of the first lights of a fall morn, signifying the start of a new dawn.

insects chirp on the branches of a willow tree, its drooping arms sheltering the swarm of children that rest beneath its shade after hours of exuberance under the scorching sun, muttering incoherent words in their jumbled excitement.

confused adolescents walk along the lakeside,
lost in self-absorbing daydreams, navigating the
complexities of the different worlds colliding in their
muddled lives, without tripping on the rundown
footpath hell bent on making them bruise their knees.

the cyan skies tincture at their clouded edges, casting
scarlet shadows that remain adamant on not blending
in with the aquamarine depths of the lake; instead
choosing to float over water like vast ships sailing in
the night.

the world all around continues to revolve, evolve and
change, but in the midst of this chaos, there flows
an infinite stream of serenity, resting upon the veins
branching across every dry leaf flying overhead in the
autumn breeze.

and perhaps, this is why fall remains golden deep
within my heart.

a yearning for the tender, carefree days of spring

cotton laden winds blow past my
verandah, pressing the perfumed
scent of budding *mogras* to their
bare chests, enticing gutsy tufts
of keratin nestled within pierced noses.

soft footsteps the size of coarsely
peeled palms press against the grass,
barefoot and glistening with saline fluids
dwelling on their soot-stained soles;
weary bodies clothed in trendy
spiderman t-shirts and mismatched
shorts wrestle on the grass,
their gleeful giggles floating like
spots of ashen dust that sink
down at sunset to rest on
pastel pink cemented banisters.

tetra packs of chilled latté and
squashed plastic soda bottles
rest far away from ultramarine bins
brimming with rotten fruit peels.
parched throats dig into musk
melons and sour litchis with a
zeal comparable to when bowls of
maggi serve as meals for the day.

bored wasps trail behind pre-
schoolers with oscillating voice
cords that sing shrill melodies,
to rouse unsuspecting parents
from their afternoon naps and
hand out hugs and crooning words
like melted milk chocolates lying
outside overworked refrigerators.

the ether adorns itself in crimson
robes in the shade of berry flavoured
lollipops to comfort drooping eyelids,
that try to conceal the fatigue
glimmering in their orbs; too hesitant
to rest despite their sorely bruised kneecaps.

dozen compromises and a sunset later,
lush backyards clear out to let the trees
resume their nightly breathing exercises,
and allow the grass to recuperate from the
liveliness of erratic playtimes;
a perpetual routine for the budding
spirits yet to encounter the struggles
of end of term examinations and
and fresh sessions every school year.

the end of the world is a scene from a movie reel

i once lost the keys to my keepsake's drawer and in search of it, i discovered a see-through wall into my home that let the world peek into my vulnerabilities. the cat i let in through my window sits on my lap as i ponder over those long nights when i cried myself to sleep only for the world to watch it as if it were a movie reel.

tuesday leaves us a little worse for wear which would explain why my hands shiver each time i pick up the pen. but persistent are these fingers that refuse to give up on half spoilt tales of mythical creatures and their bodies rotting in the woods across my backyard.

i remember the last time i met my kin; an auspicious ceremony to commemorate the existence of a life who walked for long years on this planet. fresh flowers line the funeral path, adorning it a well-worn look of love. fragile silences, flimsy people and feeble sobs ricochet in the tense atmosphere and for a moment i wonder if tomorrow was the end of the world, would people still react this way?

after all, no wars are fought for peace anymore, all we
have is a handful of mercy served on broken platters
to millions of terrified stomachs famished by fear of
things never getting better. so all we do is wait for the
day when the purgatory gates open up and wash away
the remnants of art on earth.

and when venice finally drowns, we climb onto our
roofs one last time to watch the sun set on a dying
horizon and pray for renaissance and liberty on a
paradise away from the hell we created on earth.

april showers: a soft epilogue

petrichor-laden winds caress the fresh lime green kapok leaves resting on drenched asphalt coated with alluvial mud, embracing them so they float over to where i sit on the flooded balcony with a book on my lap.

it's thursday evening, the melodious cacophony of arboreal beings echoes faintly in the background, blending into the pacifying beats of the lo-fi music playing through the unfaulty ear of my tangled earphones.

my crimson-rimmed irises are affixed on the pictures embellished on glossy one-eighty gsm sheets of the yearbook, that seem to speak in a luminescent glow, narrating tales of all the emotions i experienced throughout school.

it's been two weeks since that fateful day when i bid adieu to the comfort i've come to cherish over the past twelve years beneath the pouring skies to start a new phase, leaving behind memories i wish to hold onto forever.

i recall a popular saying that states that in order to move forward, you need to let go of even the most precious things that hold you back. but how do i let go of the world that moulded me bit by bit into the person i am today?

the truth is i am scared i will wake up one morning and forget the chalky residue outside the windows of my classroom and the scent of deep-fried junk food and sweaty uniforms at peak rush hours during lunch in the canteen.

i am terrified of change, of moving away, of leaving behind all sense of familiarity only to forget the intricate moments i associate with everything dear to me. i am scared of being left behind, of not being good enough and failing to achieve my dreams.

but i wish to grow and spread my floral wings to soar above the first clouds of the season that weep april showers. i want to fly, so i can no longer stay back and envelop myself in the solace resting in the arms of those around me.

hence, i write soft epilogues on the golden borders
of these pictures and adorn them with saline tears to
preserve the memories that bloom to life each time
i flip through the pages and hold them close to my
heart.

for with each april shower that blesses the soil,
arrives the time to say goodbye.